MW00768216

STATES

RHODE
ISLAND

A MyReportLinks.com Book

Stephen Feinstein

MyReportLinks.com Books

an imprint of
Enslow Publishers, Inc. **E**
Box 398, 40 Industrial Road
Berkeley Heights, NJ 07922
USA

MyReportLinks.com Books, an imprint of Enslow Publishers, Inc. MyReportLinks is
a trademark of Enslow Publishers, Inc.

Library of Congress Cataloging-in-Publication Data

Feinstein, Stephen.
    Rhode Island / Stephen Feinstein.
        p. cm. — (States)
Summary: Discusses the land and climate, economy, government, and
history of the state whose capital is Providence. Includes Internet
links to Web sites, source documents, and photographs related to Rhode
Island.
Includes bibliographical references and index.
    ISBN 0-7660-5028-9
 1. Rhode Island—Juvenile literature. [1. Rhode Island.] I. Title.
II. States (Series : Berkeley Heights, N.J.)
    F79.3 .F45 2003
    974.5—dc21

                    2002008996

Printed in the United States of America

10 9 8 7 6 5 4 3 2 1

To Our Readers:
Through the purchase of this book, you and your library gain access to the Report Links that specifically back
up this book.
The Publisher will provide access to the Report Links that back up this book and will keep these Report Links
up to date on **www.myreportlinks.com** for three years from the book's first publication date.
We have done our best to make sure all Internet addresses in this book were active and appropriate when we
went to press. However, the author and the Publisher have no control over, and assume no liability for, the
material available on those Internet sites or on other Web sites they may link to.
The usage of the MyReportLinks.com Books Web site is subject to the terms and conditions stated on the
Usage Policy Statement on **www.myreportlinks.com**.
In the future, a password may be required to access the Report Links that back up this book. The password
is found on the bottom of page 4 of this book.
Any comments or suggestions can be sent by e-mail to comments@myreportlinks.com or to the address on
the back cover.

Photo Credits: © Corel Corporation, pp. 3, 10; © 1995 PhotoDisc, p. 45; Enslow Publishers, Inc.,
pp. 1, 18; Library of Congress, pp. 3 (Constitution), 37; MyReportLinks.com Books, p. 4; National
Gallery of Arts, p. 16; ProvidenceRI.com, p. 33; Redwood Library, p. 39; Religious Freedom: The Trial
of Anne Hutchinson, p. 30; Rhode Island Kids' Page, pp. 24, 29; Rhode Island Tourism Division,
pp. 13, 20, 22, 26, 27, 35, 41; The Preservation Society of Newport County, p. 14; University of
Pennsylvania, p. 43.

Cover Photo: © 1995 PhotoDisc

Cover Description: Wickford Harbor, North Kingstown.

Contents

MyReportLinks.com Books
Great Books, Great Links, Great for Research!

MyReportLinks.com Books present the information you need to learn about your report subject. In addition, they show you where to go on the Internet for more information. The pre-evaluated Report Links that back up this book are kept up to date on **www.myreportlinks.com**. With the purchase of a MyReportLinks.com Books title, you and your library gain access to the Report Links that specifically back up that book. The Report Links save hours of research time and link to dozens—even hundreds—of Web sites, source documents, and photos related to your report topic.

Please see "To Our Readers" on the Copyright page for important information about this book, the MyReportLinks.com Books Web site, and the Report Links that back up this book.

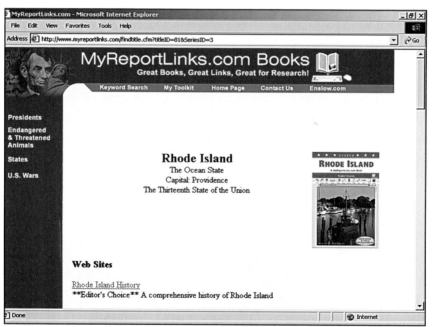

Access:

The Publisher will provide access to the Report Links that back up this book and will try to keep these Report Links up to date on our Web site for three years from the book's first publication date. Please enter **SRI2695** if asked for a password.

Report Links

 The Internet sites described below can be accessed at
http://www.myreportlinks.com

*EDITOR'S CHOICE

▶ **Rhode Island History**
From "Indians and Explorers" to "The Era of Reform," this Web site
provides a comprehensive history of Rhode Island.

Link to this Internet site from http://www.myreportlinks.com

*EDITOR'S CHOICE

▶ **Rhode Island Kids' Page**
The Rhode Island Kids' Page includes fun facts, state symbols,
a coloring book, folk stories, and a brief history of Rhode Island.

Link to this Internet site from http://www.myreportlinks.com

*EDITOR'S CHOICE

▶ **Explore the States: Rhode Island**
America's Story from America's Library, a Library of Congress Web site,
tells the story of Rhode Island. Learn local legends and facts about
the state.

Link to this Internet site from http://www.myreportlinks.com

*EDITOR'S CHOICE

▶ **Religious Freedom: The Trial of Anne Hutchinson**
This PBS Web site tells the story of Anne Hutchinson, a woman, who
in 1637, was accused of trying to overthrow the government and stood
trial for expressing her belief in religious freedom.

Link to this Internet site from http://www.myreportlinks.com

*EDITOR'S CHOICE

▶ **Today In History**
Roger Williams was banished from the Massachusetts Bay Colony.
At this Web site you will find his story of how he fought for religious
freedom and helped found the colony of Rhode Island.

Link to this Internet site from http://www.myreportlinks.com

*EDITOR'S CHOICE

▶ **U.S. Census Bureau: Rhode Island**
The U.S. Census Bureau provides quick facts about the state of Rhode
Island. Here you will learn about the businesses, geography, and people
of Rhode Island.

Link to this Internet site from http://www.myreportlinks.com

Any comments? Contact us: **comments@myreportlinks.com**   5 ▶

		STOP						
Back	Forward	Stop	Review	Home	Explore	Favorites	History

Report Links

 The Internet sites described below can be accessed at
http://www.myreportlinks.com

▶ **Colonial Charters, Grants and Related Documents**
At this Web site you will find many documents related to Rhode Island, including the state constitution.

Link to this Internet site from http://www.myreportlinks.com

▶ **Gilbert Stuart (American, 1755–1828)**
The National Gallery of Art contains the biography of Rhode Island native Gilbert Stuart. There are images of many of his paintings, including George Washington's official presidential portrait.

Link to this Internet site from http://www.myreportlinks.com

▶ **The H. P. Lovecraft Archive**
At this Web site you will learn about H. P. Lovecraft, a horror story writer and native Rhode Islander. You will find links to his writings, biographical information, and other resources.

Link to this Internet site from http://www.myreportlinks.com

▶ **Innovators: Horace Mann (1796–1859)**
This PBS biography of Horace Mann provides information about Mann, his educational philosophy, and his legacy. You will also find background about the state of the nineteenth century school system which Mann was instrumental in reforming.

Link to this Internet site from http://www.myreportlinks.com

▶ **Jack Reed—United States Senator from Rhode Island**
At this Web site you will find the biography of Senator Jack Reed. You can also read about Rhode Island's history, tourism, recreation, government, and its famous citizens.

Link to this Internet site from http://www.myreportlinks.com

▶ **Julia Ward Howe**
The Celebration of Women Writers brings you the complete text and images of a 1916 biography of Julia Ward Howe. Paintings, photographs, and her poems are also included.

Link to this Internet site from http://www.myreportlinks.com

Report Links

 The Internet sites described below can be accessed at
http://www.myreportlinks.com

▶ Leif Ericsson: Discoverer of America

Here you will find information about Viking navigator Leif Ericsson,
who many agree was the first European explorer to visit the shores of
America—perhaps even on the coast of Rhode Island.

Link to this Internet site from http://www.myreportlinks.com

▶ Newport Notables

The Redwood Library and Athenaeum holds dozens of biographies of
notable Rhode Islanders, including Julia Ward Howe and Oliver
Hazard Perry.

Link to this Internet site from http://www.myreportlinks.com

▶ Newport Mansions: The Gilded Age Experience

From the Preservation Society of Newport County you will find
pictures, articles, and visitor information about the extravagant
mansions of the Vanderbilts, the Belmonts, the Wetmores, and other
notable Newporters.

Link to this Internet site from http://www.myreportlinks.com

▶ Oliver Hazard Perry

This biography of Rhode Island native Commodore Oliver Hazard
Perry focuses on the Battle of Lake Erie during the War of 1812.
During the battle, he bravely distinguished himself as a national hero.

Link to this Internet site from http://www.myreportlinks.com

▶ PawSox

This Web site provides information about the PawSox, a minor-league
affiliate of the Boston Red Sox baseball team.

Link to this Internet site from http://www.myreportlinks.com

▶ The People and the Land: The Wampanoag of Southern New England

At this Web site you can explore the history of the Wampanoag people.

Link to this Internet site from http://www.myreportlinks.com

 The Internet sites described below can be accessed at
http://www.myreportlinks.com

▶**ProvidenceRI.com**
At this Web site you will find information about Providence, the state capital.
Click on "History & Facts" to take a tour of historic Providence City Hall.

Link to this Internet site from http://www.myreportlinks.com

▶**Rhode Island Maps**
The Perry-Castañeda Library holds a large collection of maps. Here you will
find many maps of Rhode Island, including state maps, city maps, and
historical maps.

Link to this Internet site from http://www.myreportlinks.com

▶**Rhode Island and Providence Plantations**
This Web site contains many links with information about Rhode Island.
There is also an image of the state flag and the state itself.

Link to this Internet site from http://www.myreportlinks.com

▶**Stately Knowledge: Rhode Island**
This Web site contains a listing of basic facts about Rhode Island. You will
also find links to other Internet resources.

Link to this Internet site from http://www.myreportlinks.com

▶**The Story of Samuel Slater**
At the official Slater Mill Historic Site Web site there is a biography of Samuel
Slater. Learn how he became known as the Father of American Industry.

Link to this Internet site from http://www.myreportlinks.com

▶**Today In History**
At this Web site you will find the congratulatory address written by Moses
Seixas to George Washington regarding the free and equal status of Jewish-
American citizens.

Link to this Internet site from http://www.myreportlinks.com

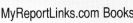

▶ **Today In History: Julia Ward Howe**
Here you will learn about many of Julia Ward Howe's accomplishments, including her composition "The Battle Hymn of the Republic."

Link to this Internet site from http://www.myreportlinks.com

▶ **Visit Rhode Island**
At this Web site you will find information about beaches, historic sites, museums, and travel. You can also learn about the economy, geography, government, history, state symbols, and other state facts.

Link to this Internet site from http://www.myreportlinks.com

▶ **Voting Rights and the Dorr Rebellion**
This article which discusses the Dorr Rebellion, during which time working people demanded the right to vote.

Link to this Internet site from http://www.myreportlinks.com

▶ **Welcome to Touro Synagogue**
At the Touro Synagogue Web site you can read about this historic building and the congregation which it houses. You can also view pictures and read a letter from George Washington to the congregation guaranteeing them religious liberty.

Link to this Internet site from http://www.myreportlinks.com

▶ **Who was Commodore Whipple?**
This biography of Commodore Abraham Whipple discusses his involvement with the Gaspee affair, his victory in the first official naval battle of the Revolutionary War, and many more of his outstanding accomplishments as both a seaman and a soldier.

Link to this Internet site from http://www.myreportlinks.com

▶ **Yale, Slavery, & Abolition: Samuel Hopkins**
Here you will find an article about Reverend Samuel Hopkins' abolitionist beliefs. Also, make sure to click the Ezra Stiles link to learn more about Hopkins' fellow Newport Congregationalist minister who also opposed slavery.

Link to this Internet site from http://www.myreportlinks.com

Capital
Providence

Gained Statehood
May 29, 1790,
the thirteenth state.

Counties
5

Population
1,048,319*

Bird
Rhode Island Red chicken

Tree
Red maple

Flower
Violet

Shell
Quahog

Mineral
Bowenite

Stone
Cumberlandite

Song
"Rhode Island's It for Me,"
words by Charlie Hall, music by
Maria Day.

March
"Rhode Island," words and music
by T. Clarke Brown.

Population reflects the 2000 census.

Motto
"Hope"

Nicknames
Ocean State; Little Rhody

Flag
The white background symbolizes
the Rhode Island soldiers who
lost their lives in the American
Revolution. There is a gold anchor,
a symbol of hope, in the center of
the flag. Beneath the anchor is a
blue ribbon inscribed with the
word "Hope" in gold letters. A
circle formed by thirteen gold stars
surround the anchor and ribbon.
The thirteen stars represent the
thirteen original colonies.

Seal
In the center of the circular seal is
a golden anchor with the word
"Hope" above it. A border around
the anchor reads: "Seal of the State
of Rhode Island and Providence
Plantations 1636." The date 1636
is the year Roger Williams founded
Providence, Rhode Island's first
permanent European settlement.

The State of Rhode Island

Rhode Island is the smallest state, tiny compared with most other states. It covers only 1,045 square miles. Rhode Island was the first of the thirteen original colonies to declare independence from Great Britain. The state's traditions of political and religious liberty became key elements in the United States Constitution. Later, Rhode Island became the birthplace of America's Industrial Revolution.

▶ What is in a Name?

Although it is sometimes called "Little Rhody," Rhode Island has the longest official name of any state—Rhode Island and Providence Plantations. The state's name is also interesting because Rhode Island is not an island. Historians have different explanations for how the state got its name. Some believe Italian navigator Giovanni da Verrazano was responsible. In 1524, Verrazano gave the name Rhode Island to what would later be called Block Island, a small island south of the state. It apparently reminded him of the Greek island of Rhodes in the Mediterranean Sea. Others believe the name originated with the Dutch explorer Adriaen Block. In 1614, Block noticed red clay soil on the shore of an island in Narragansett Bay. He named the island Roodt Eylandt (Red Island) and this later this became the name of the whole region.

In 1636, Roger Williams founded a settlement on the mainland and called it Providence. It was located on the

Seekonk River, just north of Narragansett Bay. In 1644, the settlement of farmers received a charter from the British Parliament. In the charter, the settlement was named the Providence Plantations in Narragansett Bay. Meanwhile, the island of Aquidneck, the largest in Narragansett Bay, was officially named Rhode Island.

In 1663, a second charter was issued, naming the settlements the Colony of Rhode Island and Providence Plantations. When the colony became a state, the name was simply changed to the State of Rhode Island and Providence Plantations.

▶ The Ocean State

"Little Rhody" may be tiny, but a surprising amount of variety is packed within its borders. On the coast there are craggy cliffs, grass-covered bluffs, salt ponds, and sandy beaches. Inland there are coastal lowlands, lakes, meadows, woods, and rugged hills. Historic towns dot the coast and river valleys.

The population is also diverse. Most Rhode Islanders trace their roots back to Ireland, Italy, and French Canada. Large numbers are descendants of immigrants from southern and eastern Europe. The state's ethnic mix also includes African Americans, Narragansett Indians, Hispanic Americans from Caribbean countries, and refugees from Southeast Asia.

Rhode Island is also called the "Ocean State," even though only 40 miles of its 384-mile coastline borders the ocean. The rest borders on the state's bays, inlets, peninsulas, and islands. The Atlantic Ocean has played an important role in the development of Rhode Island. The state's deepwater ports became shipping and trading centers. Commercial fishing and whaling were also important

▲ *South Country Beach is just one of Rhode Island's many beaches.*

industries. These developments led to the growth of the state's shipbuilding industry.

Rhode Island was also the birthplace of the United States Navy. Founded in 1775 as the Continental Navy, the Navy has always had a strong presence in Rhode Island. The Navy maintains training and construction facilities in the state. Several ships are based in Newport. Visitors to Rhode Island can learn about the history of the Navy at the Naval War College Museum in Newport.

The ocean is also the main reason millions of vacationers visit Rhode Island each summer. The state's beautiful beaches, harbors, and seaside towns are a magnet for tourists. The most popular forms of recreation are boating, fishing, surfing, and swimming. Boating fans love Newport, which is known as the sailing capital of the world. From 1930 to 1983, the America's Cup yacht races

were held in the waters off Newport. The International Tennis Hall of Fame is also in Newport, and summer visitors to the town can enjoy the annual JVC Jazz Festival and other music festivals.

▶ The Gilded Age

During the late 1800s, America's wealthiest people—whose fortunes had been built on coal, oil, finance, and railroads—enjoyed displaying their wealth. It was an era known as the Gilded Age.

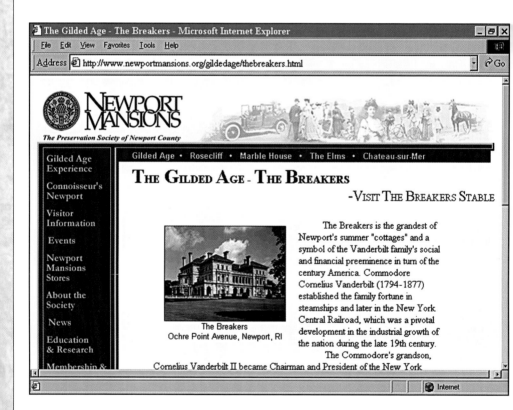

The Breakers was purchased by Cornelius Vanderbilt II in 1885, but when it was destroyed by a fire in 1892, he commissioned a new version to be built the following year. The mansion is one of many located in Newport, Rhode Island.

In Newport, the Vanderbilts, Astors, and others built spectacular palaces overlooking the ocean. They spent their summers there and held extravagant balls and dinners. They spared no expense in creating their "summer cottages." Beechwood, the Breakers, Chateau-sur-Mer, the Elms, Marble House, and Rosecliff were some of the famous "cottages." The Breakers, which belonged to shipping magnate Cornelius Vanderbilt, was a four-story limestone palace with seventy rooms, including a two-story ballroom. The mansions were filled with priceless antique furniture and works of art. Some of the most famous mansions are now museums and visitors can take guided tours through them.

Even in the Gilded Age, not everyone approved of this extravagance. The writer Henry James called the elaborate mansions "grotesque" and "white elephants."[1]

Rhode Islanders to Remember

Many outstanding men and women were either born in Rhode Island or made the state their home. Rhode Island's story began with colonial leader and clergyman Roger Williams (1603–83), who founded Providence in 1636. In 1638, religious leader Anne Hutchinson (1591–1643) helped establish Portsmouth on Aquidneck Island.

The naval commander and war hero, Oliver Hazard Perry (1785–1819), was born in South Kingstown. During the War of 1812, Perry defeated a British fleet in the Battle of Lake Erie. He is remembered for the famous words he wrote during the heat of battle, "We have met the enemy, and they are ours."[2]

The painter Gilbert Stuart (1755–1828), born in North Kingstown, is best known for his famous portrait of George Washington. Samuel Slater (1768–1835), the father of the American textile industry, built the nation's

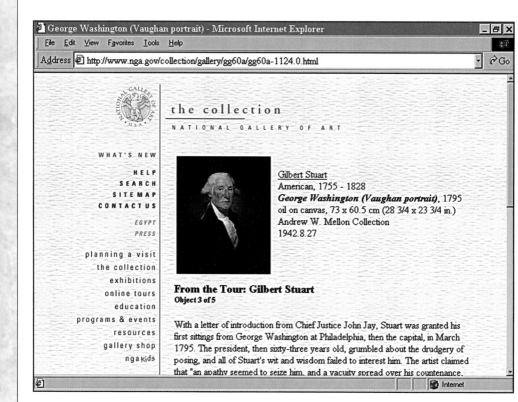

the collection

NATIONAL GALLERY OF ART

WHAT'S NEW

HELP
SEARCH
SITEMAP
CONTACT US

EGYPT
PRESS

planning a visit
the collection
exhibitions
online tours
education
programs & events
resources
gallery shop
nga Kids

Gilbert Stuart
American, 1755 - 1828
George Washington (Vaughan portrait), 1795
oil on canvas, 73 x 60.5 cm (28 3/4 x 23 3/4 in.)
Andrew W. Mellon Collection
1942.8.27

From the Tour: Gilbert Stuart
Object 3 of 5

With a letter of introduction from Chief Justice John Jay, Stuart was granted his first sittings from George Washington at Philadelphia, then the capital, in March 1795. The president, then sixty-three years old, grumbled about the drudgery of posing, and all of Stuart's wit and wisdom failed to interest him. The artist claimed that "an apathy seemed to seize him, and a vacuity spread over his countenance

▲ *Gilbert Stuart painted this famous portrait of then-President George Washington in 1795.*

first water-powered cotton-spinning mill in Pawtucket. Horace Mann (1796–1859), a graduate of Brown University in Providence, is known as the father of American public education.

The writer and poet Julia Ward Howe (1819–1910) lived in Portsmouth and Newport. She was a reformer who championed women's rights and the abolition of slavery. She wrote the words to "The Battle Hymn of the Republic." Author Howard Phillips (H. P.) Lovecraft (1890–1937), known for his horror stories, lived and worked in Providence. Oliver Hazard Perry La Farge

(1901–63), who lived in South County, published novels and anthropological works on American Indian life. La Farge won the 1930 Pulitzer Prize for his novel *Laughing Boy.* Novelist Edwin O'Connor (1918–68), born in Providence, won the Pulitzer Prize for his novel *The Edge of Sadness* in 1962. His other novels include *All in the Family* and *The Last Hurrah.*

The statesman John Milton Hay (1838–1905) was a graduate of Brown University. He served as United States secretary of state from 1898 to 1905 and is remembered for his role in creating America's "Open Door" policy toward China.

George M. Cohan (1878–1942), born in Providence, is considered the father of American musical comedy. Among the songs he composed are "Over There," "Yankee Doodle Dandy," and "Give My Regards to Broadway."

Chapter 2

Land and Climate

Rhode Island has a total area of 1,545 square miles, including 168 square miles of inland water. The state is bordered on the north and east by Massachusetts. Connecticut lies to the west, and the Atlantic Ocean is to the south.

▶ Rhode Island's Two Regions

Rhode Island consists of two main regions—the Coastal Lowlands and the Western Rocky Upland. The Coastal

▲ A map of Rhode Island.

Lowlands forms part of a land region that extends across most of the New England coast. The Coastal Lowlands covers about two thirds of Rhode Island, including the islands in Narragansett Bay and Block Island. Narragansett Bay is an estuary—a place where seawater mixes with river water. The bay slices inland into the Coastal Lowlands region for 28 miles, nearly dividing the state into two parts. The Coastal Lowlands features sandy beaches, low coastal plains, salt ponds, salt marshes, and coastal lagoons. There are rocky cliffs on some of the islands. West of Narragansett Bay, the land gradually rises to low, forested hills.

The Western Rocky Upland is a region of rolling hills and valleys in northwestern Rhode Island. It covers about one-third of the state. It is part of the Eastern New England Upland. The highest point is 812-foot-high Jerimoth Hill. There are lakes, ponds, and reservoirs, and much of the region is forested. The main trees are ashes, birches, cedars, hemlocks, hickories, maples, oaks, pines, poplars, spruces, and willows. Almost all of Rhode Island's forests are second-growth forests, consisting of trees growing on land that was once farmland.

Rhode Island's rivers, many with waterfalls, played a major role in the development of industry in the state. Mills and factories using water as their source of power were built along the swiftly flowing rivers. The most important river was the Blackstone. Downstream, its name changes to the Pawtucket and then the Seekonk before the river flows into Narragansett Bay. The Seekonk section of the river is actually a saltwater arm of the bay, as are the Providence and Sakonnet rivers. Other important rivers in the state include the Pawcatuck and Pawtuxet.

▶ Little Rhody's Islands

Thirty-five of the state's thirty-six islands are in Narragansett Bay. The largest is Aquidneck Island (officially named Rhode Island), with an area of 45 square miles. Newport and Portsmouth are on Aquidneck Island. The town of Jamestown is on Conanicut Island. Out in the Atlantic, about 12 miles south of the Rhode Island mainland, is Block Island. Visitors can reach the 11-square-mile island by ferry. About 25 percent of Block Island's beaches, rolling hills, bluffs, coves, moors, and salt ponds are protected. Hikers on the island's nature trails can expect to see white-tailed deer and hawks. Mohegan Bluffs are spectacular 200-foot-high red clay cliffs. The

▲ Although only 40 miles of Rhode Island's borders meet the ocean, it is still referred to as the Ocean State.

historic Southeast Light lighthouse, built in 1875, sits on top of the cliffs.

▶ The Ocean's Gift

Thanks to the Atlantic Ocean and Narragansett Bay, Rhode Island enjoys a milder climate than inland states in the region. No part of Rhode Island is more than a 30-minute drive from the sea, so the entire state benefits from the ocean's moderating effect on temperatures. This means that winters in the state are not as cold or snowy as they would otherwise be. Nor are summers quite as hot as they might be. Rhode Island has an average January temperature of 29°F. The average temperature in July is 71°F. The coldest temperature ever recorded in the state was −23°F, which occurred at Kingston on January 11, 1942. On August 2, 1975, the state's hottest temperature, 104°F, was recorded at Providence.

Average annual precipitation is 44 inches. About 31 inches of snow falls each winter (10 inches of snow equals about one inch of rain). Snow along the coast often turns to rain because of the warming influence of the sea.

Being so close to the ocean is not always a blessing. In winter, ferocious coastal storms known as "nor'easters" can bring damaging winds and snow, sleet, or freezing rain. Yet there are even worse storms. Rhode Island was hit by destructive hurricanes in 1815, 1938, 1944, and 1954. The hurricane of 1938 was an especially disastrous storm. It killed 258 people in Rhode Island and caused $100 million in property damage.

Chapter 3

Economy

In 1790, Samuel Slater built the nation's first water-powered cotton mill in Pawtucket, Rhode Island. That was the beginning of America's Industrial Revolution. For more than a hundred years, Rhode Island's economy was driven by thriving manufacturing industries. At the height of industrial development, more than half of the state's workers were employed in factories.

Shipbuilding had become an important industry in Rhode Island by the early 1700s. Many Rhode Islanders were

▲ *Slater Mill, built by Samuel Slater in 1790, was the first water-powered cotton mill in the country.*

involved in fishing, overseas trade, and whaling, and there was a growing demand for ships. Fortunately, plenty of wood for building ships was available in Rhode Island's forests.

Over time, the economic landscape of Rhode Island changed. Shipbuilding remained an important industry, but early in the twentieth century many textile mills moved to the South, where labor costs were lower.

Another early industry in Rhode Island was jewelry making. It grew in importance after Nehemiah Dodge developed a method of plating cheaper metals with gold in 1794. Jewelry making is now the state's most important manufacturing industry. Providence is a leading center of the craft. There are more than a thousand manufacturers of jewelry and silverware in the state, employing more than twenty-five thousand people.[1] Costume jewelry is especially important.

Riches of the Land and Sea

In the last twenty years of the twentieth century, many factories in Rhode Island closed. Only 15 percent of Rhode Island's workers are employed in manufacturing today.

About three quarters of Rhode Island's workers are now employed in the service industries. The most important services are finance, insurance, real estate, and businesses related to tourism.

What has become of the early economic mainstays—agriculture and fishing? After all, Rhode Island is the home of the Rhode Island red chicken. This famous breed was developed in Little Compton in the 1850s. Rhode Island Reds are still raised in Rhode Island, but agriculture has declined in importance since the 1800s. Today, income from agriculture is only one percent of Rhode Island's economy, employing one percent of the state's workers.

The State Bird

▲ *The red chicken is Rhode Island's state bird.*

Much of Rhode Island's former farmland is once again covered by forest. However, Rhode Island still has more than seven hundred farms. The leading crops are potatoes, hay, and apples. Production of milk is also important.

Fishing was always an important industry in Rhode Island. New England's waters contain a wealth of marine life—fish, mollusks, and shellfish. These waters, however, were eventually in danger of being overfished. In 1976, the federal government passed a law that banned foreign vessels from fishing within 200 miles of America's shores. Rhode Island fisherman Jake Dykstra, head of the Point Judith Fishermen's Co-op, was an important supporter of

this law. The government also put limits on the size of the annual catch for certain species. Even so, the state's commercial catch totals about $80 million each year. Rhode Island's fishing boats bring in lobster, quahogs (thick-shelled clams), scallops, squid, cod, flounder, whiting, yellowfish, and many other species.

▶ Tourism

Tourism is now Rhode Island's most important industry. In 1969, the completion of the Newport Bridge and Interstate 95 through Rhode Island made the state more accessible. Since then, the number of tourists has grown dramatically. Fifteen million people visit the state each year and tourism contributes about $1.25 billion a year to Rhode Island's economy.

Rhode Island's greatest attraction is the seashore, but there is also a wealth of historic attractions. In old mill towns such as Pawtucket and Woonsocket, the textile mills are coming to life again. Slater's Mill, which stopped producing cloth in 1905, is now a museum. New bicycle paths and historic walkways have been built to draw tourists.

Amazingly, for such a small state, Rhode Island contains 20 percent of the country's National Historic Landmarks. There are more restored colonial and Victorian buildings in Rhode Island than in any other state. Providence's cobblestoned Benefit Street is known as the "Mile of History." It is lined with more than two hundred restored historic buildings of the eighteenth and nineteenth centuries. In Newport, tourists can visit Redwood Library (built in 1747), the nation's oldest library building in continuous use. They can also stop at the White Horse Tavern (opened in 1673), the oldest tavern in America.

▲ *Built in Newport in 1763, the Touro Synagogue is the country's oldest synagogue.*

Rhode Island is also important to America's religious history. The First Baptist Meeting House (1775) in Providence is the oldest Baptist church in America. The nation's oldest synagogue is the Touro Synagogue (1763) in Newport. Also in Newport is the Friends Meeting House (1699), the nation's oldest Quaker meeting house.

Government

On May 29, 1790, the State of Rhode Island and Providence Plantations became the last of the thirteen original colonies to join the Union. It thus became the thirteenth state of the new American nation.

▶ Rhode Island's Constitution

In 1663, Britain had granted a charter to the colony of Rhode Island. It was called the Charter of Rhode Island and Providence Plantations and it contained the laws for governing the colony. This royal charter continued to serve

⬛ Providence is the state capital of Rhode Island.

as Rhode Island's constitution when the colony became a state more than a hundred years later. It would later be changed time and again with the changing needs and priorities of Rhode Island's growing population.

According to the 1663 charter, only landholders or their eldest sons were eligible to vote. Although, by the 1800s, Rhode Island was a very different place from the Rhode Island of the 1600s. It was no longer a mainly agricultural society. By 1840, most Rhode Islanders lived in industrial towns and cities. They did not own land and therefore could not vote—so they demanded a voice in government.

Thomas Dorr, a Providence lawyer, formed the People's Party and led a movement to form a new state government. At the People's Convention in 1841, Dorr's followers drew up a proposed constitution granting voting rights to all adult males. The People's Party elected Dorr governor in its own special election. The so-called Dorr Rebellion failed, but it led to the new state constitution of 1843.

Under the new constitution, any native-born Rhode Island man could vote. All that was required was payment of $1 a year in taxes or service in the military.

The Rhode Island Constitution spells out the procedures for making amendments to the constitution. First, an amendment is proposed in the state legislature, which is the law-making branch of government. Amendments must be approved by a majority of the legislators and then by at least three fifths of the voters in a general election. Rhode Islanders have amended their constitution forty-two times.

Another way to amend the constitution is through a constitutional convention. To call such a convention, a majority vote by both the legislators and the voters is required. When an amendment is proposed by a constitutional convention, the change must be approved by a majority of the voters in a regular election.

The Structure of Rhode Island's Government

Rhode Island's government is based on a separation of powers like that of the federal government and the other states. There are three branches—the executive, legislative, and judicial. The executive branch carries out the laws, the legislative branch makes the laws, and the judicial branch interprets the laws.

Rhode Island's chief executive is the governor. The governor is elected to a four-year term and may be reelected

▲ The violet is Rhode Island's state flower.

29

two more times. The lieutenant governor, attorney general, secretary of state, and state treasurer are also elected to four-year terms. The governor's cabinet consists of the directors of administration, business regulation, labor and training, health, transportation, human resources, and environmental management. Most of these key officials are appointed by the governor, with the approval of the state senate.

The legislative branch of Rhode Island's government is known as the General Assembly. It consists of a fifty-member senate and a hundred-member house of

The American Experience | WayBack: Stand Up For Your Rights | Features/Religious Freedom - Microso...

File Edit View Favorites Tools Help

Address http://www.pbs.org/wgbh/amex/kids/civilrights/features_hutchison.html Go

FEATURES Stand up for your Rights **WayBack**

BUZZ   SNAPSHOT   GAME SPACE   WHO'S WHO ?

▸ WOMEN and THE VOTE ▸ SCHOOL DESEGREGATION

RELIGIOUS FREEDOM:

The Trial of Anne Hutchinson

Anne Hutchinson stood trial alone, with no lawyer to defend her. She faced a panel of 49 powerful and well-educated men. She was accused of sedition, or trying to overthrow the government. And she faced banishment if convicted.

Hutchinson's "crime" was expressing religious beliefs that were different from the colony's rulers. In the year 1637, in Massachusetts Bay Colony, that was against the law--especially for a woman.

Hutchinson, a Puritan, came to America in search of a place where she could worship freely. But when she arrived, she found the Bay Colony's religious rules very intolerant. The ideas she brought with

http://www.pbs.org/wgbh/amex/kids/civilrights/index.html   Internet

▲ Anne Hutchinson was put on trial for expressing religious ideas contradicting those of the Massachusetts Bay Colony. Upon being found guilty, she was exiled to Rhode Island. She lives on in history as a symbol of religious freedom.

representatives. Senators and representatives are elected to two-year terms.

The judicial branch consists of the state supreme court, superior court, district court, and family court. The supreme court has five justices—the chief justice and four associate justices. The General Assembly elects the justices and chooses a chief justice from among the associates. The governor appoints district, family, and superior court judges, with the approval of the senate.

Direct Democracy in Rhode Island's Local Governments

Rhode Island towns hold town meetings that are an example of direct democracy in action. The tradition of the town meeting dates back to New England's colonial days. Citizens meet, discuss important issues, and vote on a variety of matters. They elect officials, approve budgets, pass laws, and decide other town business. United States citizens who have lived in Rhode Island for at least thirty days are eligible to vote. Rhode Islanders must stay informed about local politics for this form of direct democracy to work well.

History

The first Rhode Islanders were descendants of nomadic hunters who migrated from Asia to North America during the last Ice Age. Beginning about twelve thousand years ago, various groups of these hunters had spread far and wide throughout the Americas. Some eventually reached the eastern shores of North America. The first people to enter what is now Rhode Island arrived from the west sometime between 10,000 and 9,000 B.C. The Ice Age was ending and the warming climate brought changes to the natural environment.

▷ American Indian Peoples of Rhode Island

The first inhabitants of Rhode Island, known as Paleo-Indians, had to adapt to these changing conditions. Many of the large animals they had hunted, such as the mammoth, disappeared. So they lived on small game, fish, and various berries and plants. Over time, the Paleo-Indians learned to grow their own food and they settled in villages. The land and waters provided more than enough food for their needs. The American Indians raised corn, beans, and squash. They caught fish and shellfish in the sea, salt ponds, bays, and rivers. They hunted deer, rabbit, and other animals in the forests.

By the time the first European explorers arrived in the 1500s, five main groups of American Indians lived in what is now Rhode Island—the Narragansett, Niantic, Nipmuck, Pequot, and Wampanoag. Just as in other areas, the arrival

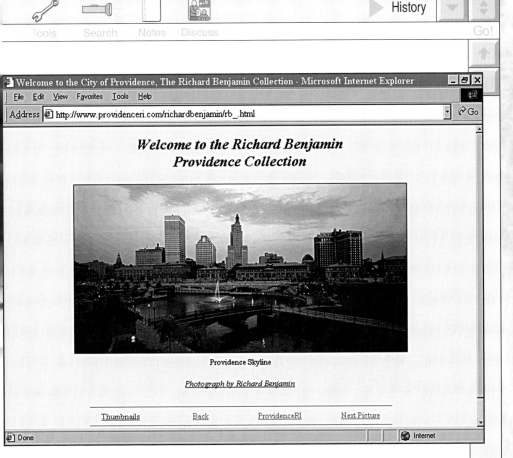

Welcome to the City of Providence, The Richard Benjamin Collection - Microsoft Internet Explorer

File   Edit   View   Favorites   Tools   Help

Address 🔲 http://www.providenceri.com/richardbenjamin/rb_.html

Welcome to the Richard Benjamin Providence Collection

Providence Skyline

Photograph by Richard Benjamin

| Thumbnails | Back | ProvidenceRI | Next Picture |

Done   🌐 Internet

▲ *Roger Williams purchased the area now known as Providence from the Narragansett Indians. He settled the land in June 1636. Today, Providence is the capital of Rhode Island.*

of the Europeans proved to be a disaster for the American Indians of Rhode Island.

▶ European Explorers and Settlers

The first Europeans to visit the area may have been Vikings from Norway. Leif Eriksson is believed to have reached the shores of North America in the year A.D. 1000. He found grapes growing there and named the area Vinland. The Vikings referred to the natives of Vinland as *skrellings* (Norse for "dwarfs").

Historians disagree about the location of Vinland. Some point farther north, to places such as Newfoundland or Nova Scotia. Others think the Vikings may have landed as far south as Massachusetts. Some people believe that a stone tower in Newport, Rhode Island, known as the Old Stone Mill, was actually built by the Vikings. At any rate, the Vikings did not stay long in North America.

Italian explorer Giovanni da Verrazano explored Narragansett Bay in 1524. Nearly one hundred years later, the Dutch explorer Adriaen Block visited the same area. Meanwhile, the British had become interested in establishing colonies in the New World. King James I granted the Plymouth Company a charter for settlement in North America.

In 1616, John Smith, a surveyor for the Plymouth Company, explored New England. Smith apparently liked what he saw. In his report, he wrote,

> And surely by reason of those sandy cliffes and cliffes of rocks, both which we saw so planted with Gardens and Corne fields, and so well inhabited with a goodly, strong and well proportioned people, besides the greatnesse of the Timber growing on Them, the greatnesse of the fish and moderate temper of the ayre . . . who can but approve this a most excellent place, both for health & fertility? And of all the four parts of the world that I have seen not inhabited, could I have but means to transport a Colonie, I would rather live here than anywhere. . . .[1]

At that time, the Church of England did not tolerate other religious beliefs. Seeking freedom from persecution, a group of English Puritans looked for a new home. They made a deal with the Plymouth Company to finance a settlement in North America. In 1620, this group, known as the Pilgrims, set sail from Plymouth, England, aboard the

Mayflower. They established the Plymouth Colony in what is now Massachusetts. Other groups of Puritans seeking religious freedom soon followed them across the ocean and established communities throughout New England. The Puritans in North America could now enjoy their own religion without interference. Yet the Puritans themselves proved to be intolerant of anyone with different religious ideas.

The Reverend Roger Williams, who arrived in Salem in 1630, was a strong believer in religious tolerance. He also believed that the church should not be involved in government affairs, and vice versa. In 1636, in Salem, Williams preached that "forced worship stinks in God's nostrils."[2]

The Puritan leaders decided to send Williams back to England because of his beliefs. When he learned about this, Williams, his wife, and some friends fled into the wilderness. They ended up in what is now Rhode Island. There, Williams founded the colony of Providence on land given to him by two friendly Narragansett Indian chiefs called Canonicus and Miantonomi.

▲ The First Baptist Church is the oldest Baptist church in the country.

Others soon joined Williams in exile, including Anne Hutchinson, a religious reformer who had been banished from Massachusetts. They established the settlements of Portsmouth, Newport, and Warwick.

With Roger Williams as governor, the colony of Rhode Island became known as a place where people could worship as they pleased. A group of Quakers arrived in Newport in 1657, and a group of Jewish people from Spain and Portugal arrived in Newport in 1658. Williams's own religious beliefs were constantly changing. After founding America's first Baptist congregation, Williams left it to follow God's will as a "Seeker."

Rhode Island's royal charter of 1663, granted by King Charles II of Britain, guaranteed the colony's status as an "experiment" in religious freedom. The charter spelled out the colony's purpose: "To hold forth a lively experiment that a most flourishing civil state may stand and best be main-tained with full liberty in religious concernments."[3] The charter also granted the right of self-government. Rhode Island thus became the first American colony to freely elect its own government—America's first democracy.

▶ King Philip's War

Unlike most of the European settlers in New England, Roger Williams had deep respect for the native people. He believed the settlers had no right to the natives' land unless the American Indians had agreed to a legal transfer of property. Williams studied the American Indian customs and learned their language. He wrote a book about the Algonquian language called *A Key into the Language of America*. Unfortunately, most of the colonists were more interested in gaining the American Indians' lands than in winning their friendship. More and more settlers moved

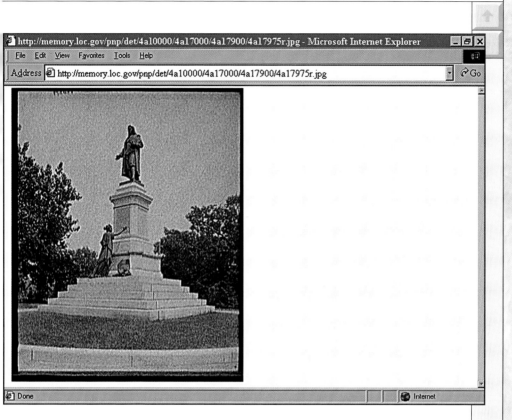

```
http://memory.loc.gov/pnp/det/4a10000/4a17000/4a17900/4a17975r.jpg - Microsoft Internet Explorer
File  Edit  View  Favorites  Tools  Help
Address  http://memory.loc.gov/pnp/det/4a10000/4a17000/4a17900/4a17975r.jpg          Go
Done                                                                    Internet
```

▲ Rhode Island became America's first democracy. This statue of Roger Williams pays tribute to the state's first governor and proponent of a democratic society.

onto American Indian lands. The American Indians came to believe that they had no choice but to fight to protect their territory.

In 1675, the Wampanoag chief Metacomet, called King Philip by the settlers, called on the tribes to unite. Led by Metacomet, the Wampanoag, Narragansett, and other tribes began attacking settlers. However, the American Indians were outnumbered about five to one by the colonial fighters. Old differences of opinion divided the tribes and made it difficult for Metacomet to maintain

unity among them. The tragic climax of King Philip's War occurred on December 19, 1675, in the Great Swamp Fight. Colonists attacked a Narragansett camp in a swamp near present-day Kingston, Rhode Island. About two thousand Narragansett men, women, and children were killed. Many were trapped in burning wigwams. Over the next few months, Metacomet and his warriors continued to attack European settlements. Still the Narragansett's spirit had been broken and Metacomet's forces dwindled as his men were killed in battle. Eventually Metacomet was captured. In July 1676, he was beheaded and all Wampanoag land was confiscated.

▶ "Rogue's Island"

In the late 1600s and early 1700s, Rhode Island farmers known as the Narragansett Planters established plantations similar to those in the South. Slaves did much of the field work. At the same time, the sea was increasingly becoming a source of wealth for Rhode Islanders. Newport, Providence, and Bristol became bustling seaports during the 1700s. Merchants became wealthy exporting Rhode Island's agricultural products across the ocean.

Many Rhode Island merchants took part in the Triangle Trade. Newport merchants imported molasses and sugar from the West Indies. The molasses and sugar were used to make rum. The merchants shipped kegs of rum to West Africa, trading them for African slaves. The Africans were shipped to the West Indies, where they were sold into slavery in exchange for molasses and sugar. Finally, the molasses, sugar, and any remaining slaves were shipped back to the American colonies. The sugar and molasses were used to make more rum. Rhode Island merchants grew extremely wealthy through this trading.

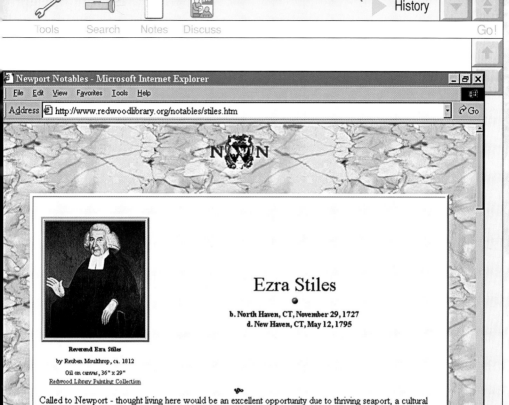

Ezra Stiles

b. North Haven, CT, November 29, 1727
d. New Haven, CT, May 12, 1795

Reverend Ezra Stiles
by Reuben Moulthrop, ca. 1812
Oil on canvas, 36" x 29"
Redwood Library Painting Collection

Called to Newport - thought living here would be an excellent opportunity due to thriving seaport, a cultural center, and the Redwood Library. Ordained as pastor of Second Congregational Church on October 22, 1755, beginning 20 year residency here.

Reverend Ezra Stiles was an advocate of liberty, including that of African Americans. He strongly supported the American Revolution. Stiles was also in support of education as he played a large role in founding Brown University and served as president of Yale University.

Some Rhode Islanders opposed slavery. To them, the idea of denying people their freedom was especially intolerable in a colony founded on individual freedom. Samuel Hopkins and Ezra Stiles helped enact a ban on slave trading in Rhode Island in 1774. It was the first such law in the colonies.

Some Rhode Island sea captains found another source of wealth—the cargoes of ships of other nations. They worked for the British government as "privateers." During the 1700s, Britain fought a series of wars with Holland,

Spain, and France. The job of the privateers was to capture and disable enemy ships at sea. In the process, the privateers looted the cargo of the ships. Their actions were hard to distinguish from outright piracy. Meanwhile, residents of Block Island helped themselves to the cargoes of ships that had been wrecked on the rocks and sandbars around the island. This activity became so profitable that some islanders actually helped to cause more wrecks. They set up lanterns and flares at night to confuse the ships. Before long, Rhode Island had earned the nickname "Rogue's Island."

▶ The Revolutionary War

During the 1700s, Britain passed laws putting restrictions on trade in the American colonies. The British goal was to make sure that wealth from the colonies went home to Britain. For example, there were laws forbidding the manufacture of woolen goods and hats. The colonists were therefore forced to buy these from Britain.

In 1733, Britain passed the Molasses Act, placing taxes on the import of molasses into the colonies. Rhode Island merchants needed molasses for the Triangle Trade but they did not want to pay the high taxes. They decided to smuggle the molasses instead and hired privateers to keep them supplied.

Eventually, Britain began to crack down on smugglers and tax evaders. In 1763, British patrol ships stopped and searched vessels in Rhode Island's harbors. Shipments of illegal molasses were confiscated. In 1764, the Sugar Act added new restrictions on the import of sugar and molasses. The following year, the Stamp Act further outraged the colonists by taxing paper items such as newspapers, playing cards, and legal documents.

This was the last straw. The colonists, especially Rhode Islanders, took action. On June 4, 1765, a group of angry Rhode Islanders in Newport set fire to a boat from the Royal Navy ship *Maidstone*. Then, in 1769, another British ship, the *Liberty*, was burned at Newport. On June 9, 1772, Providence merchant John Brown led an attack on the British schooner *Gaspee*, which had run aground. The *Gaspee*'s captain was wounded and the ship was burned. Other acts of defiance occurred elsewhere. In Massachusetts, the famous Boston Tea Party was an angry response to the Tea Act of 1773. Bostonians climbed aboard a British ship and dumped its cargo of tea into Boston Harbor.

▲ Although May 4 is Rhode Island's Independence Day, it is at a July 4 parade that people celebrate the nation's declaration of independence from Great Britain over two hundred years ago.

The growing tensions between Britain and its American colonies eventually resulted in war. In 1774, the Continental Congress, consisting of delegates from the thirteen colonies, met in Philadelphia. The delegates appointed George Washington as commander-in-chief of the Continental Army. Washington chose Nathanael Greene of Warwick, Rhode Island, as his second-in-command. Esek Hopkins of Providence was appointed commander-in-chief of the Continental Navy, which did not yet exist.

On April 18, 1775, the American Revolution began in Concord, Massachusetts, when fighting broke out between colonists and British troops. Rhode Island's general assembly appointed Captain Abraham Whipple to command two warships, the first American navy. On May 4, 1776, two months before the signing of the Declaration of Independence, Rhode Island became the first colony to declare its independence from Britain. Since 1884, May 4 has been celebrated as Rhode Island Independence Day.

During the war, British troops occupied Newport from December 1776 to October 1779. In 1778, the Battle of Rhode Island occurred at Newport and Portsmouth. Rhode Island's 1st Black Regiment, consisting of former slaves, fought bravely. The colonists, though, were unable to drive out the British. By the time the British left Newport, much of the town had been destroyed.

The Revolutionary War ended in 1783. By 1790, twelve of the thirteen original American colonies had become states of the new American nation. Rhode Island was the first colony to declare its independence, but was reluctant to sign the U.S. Constitution. Rhode Island had a long tradition of respect for individual freedoms. Thus, Rhode Islanders worried about entrusting their rights and

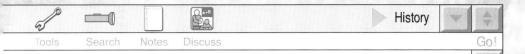

freedoms to a powerful federal government. An agreement was reached to add a group of amendments, known as the Bill of Rights, to the Constitution. The amendments guaranteed individual liberties. They also placed limits on the powers of the federal government. Only then did Rhode Island agree to ratify the Constitution.

An Industrial Powerhouse

Not long after the American Revolution had ended, the nation's Industrial Revolution began. At the forefront of this revolution was the Rhode Island town of Pawtucket, located on the Blackstone River. In 1790, Providence

Julia Ward Howe first published "The Battle Hymn of the Republic" as a poem in February 1862. It later became a song sung by union troops during the Civil War.

merchant Moses Brown hired Samuel Slater to work for him at his cotton-spinning mill in Pawtucket.

Slater had worked at textile mills in Britain. There he had used the Arkwright machine, a water-powered spinning machine. The Arkwright process was a closely guarded industrial secret in Britain and no one with knowledge of the Arkwright process was allowed to leave the country. Slater managed to escape, claiming to be a farmer. At Brown's mill in Pawtucket, Slater built the water-powered machines of the Arkwright system from memory.

The textile industry expanded rapidly in Rhode Island as other mills were built on the Blackstone and other rivers. There were several reasons for the success of textiles in Rhode Island: abundance of water power, the use of power spinning machines, and nearby markets in Boston and New York. In addition to textiles, Rhode Island factories also produced metal tools and equipment. Beginning in the 1820s, waves of immigrants arrived in Rhode Island to work in the mills. Entire families, including young children, worked in conditions that often were unhealthy and dangerous. Workers formed labor unions to win better working conditions.

During the Civil War (1861–65), more than twenty-four thousand Rhode Islanders fought for the Union. Among them was Major General Ambrose Burnside, who later served as governor of Rhode Island and as a United States senator. Burnside was famous for his bushy whiskers, which became known as "sideburns."

▶ The Twentieth Century

The twentieth century brought a reversal of fortune for Rhode Island's mighty textile industry. Lower costs of

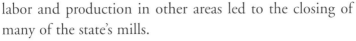
labor and production in other areas led to the closing of many of the state's mills.

The two world wars brought industrial work to the state. During World War I (1914–18), chemicals, munitions, combat ships, and cargo ships were produced. During World War II (1939–45), Rhode Island factories made torpedoes and prefabricated, sheet-metal Quonset huts. In the 1980s, Rhode Island industries benefited again from a national defense buildup. By the end of the century, though, Rhode Island was no longer an industrial powerhouse.

Tourism has become Rhode Island's main focus. The state's historic sites, music festivals, beaches, and fresh seafood attract many visitors. Others come for museums and mansions, or for yachts and ships. By focusing on its rich history, natural beauty, and water resources, Rhode Island has become a great place to live and visit.

▲ The state's bays, harbors, and lakes are a reason why tourists are attracted to Rhode Island. Its beautiful waters are a great place to go sailing, fishing, or to just soak up the sun's rays.

Chapter Notes

Chapter 1. The State of Rhode Island

1. Henry James, as quoted in Phyllis Méras and Tom Gannon, *Rhode Island: An Explorer's Guide* (Woodstock, Vt.: The Countryman Press, 1995), p. 153.

2. Richard Dillon, *We Have Met the Enemy: Oliver Hazard Perry, Wilderness Commodore* (New York: McGraw-Hill Book Company, 1978), p. 153.

Chapter 3. Economy

1. RIEDC, "The Jewelry Industry: A part of history, a partnership for the future," *Rhode Island Economic Development Corporation,* n.d., <http://www.riedc.com/cluster/jewelry_industry/Jewelry.htm> (October 2, 2002).

Chapter 5. History

1. John Smith in his Description of New England (1616), as quoted in Susan Gordon, ed., *New England* (London: Insight Guides, 2000), p. 26.

2. Ibid., p. 29.

3. John B. Harwood, "A Lively Experiment," *Rhode Island General Assembly,* n.d., <http://www.riln.state.ri.us/greeting.html> (October 3, 2002).

Further Reading

Aylesworth, Thomas G. *Southern New England: Connecticut, Massachusetts, Rhode Island.* Broomall, Pa.: Chelsea House Publishers, 1988.

Gavan, Terrence. *The Barons of Newport: A Guide to the Gilded Age.* Newport, R.I.: Pineapple Publications, 1988.

———. *Complete Guide to Newport.* Newport, R.I.: Pineapple Publications, 1988.

Gordon, Susan, ed. *New England.* London: Insight Guides, 2000.

Grant, Kim and Steve Jermanok. *New England.* Hawthorn, Vic., Australia: Lonely Planet Publications, 1999.

McDevitt, Neale, ed. *New England.* London: Dorling Kindersley Publishing, 2001.

McNair, Sylvia. *Rhode Island.* Second ed. New York: Children's Press, 2000.

Méras, Phyllis and Tom Gannon. *Rhode Island: An Explorer's Guide.* Woodstock, Vt.: The Countryman Press, 1995.

Thompson, Kathleen. *Rhode Island.* Austin, Tex.: Raintree Steck-Vaughn Publishers, 1996.

Warner, J. F. *Rhode Island.* Minneapolis, Minn.: Lerner Publications, 1993.

Weeden, William B. *Early Rhode Island: A Social History of the People, 1636–1790.* Bowie, Md.: Heritage Books, 1991.

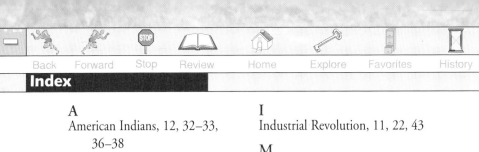